NEVER CAN SAY GOODBYE

Answers to Life's Greatest Mysteries

NEVER CAN SAY GOODBYE

Answers to Life's Greatest Mysteries

Betsey Lewis

Dragonfly Dimensions Publishing

Never Can Say Goodbye—Answers to Life's Greatest Mysteries

Softcover ISBN: 978-1-5142-2655-1

© 2015 by Betsey Lewis.

All rights reserved. No part of this book may be reproduced by any mechanical, photographic, or electronic process, or in the form of a phonographic recording; nor may it be stored in a retrieval system, transmitted, or otherwise be copied for public or private use—other than for "fair use" as brief quotations embodied in articles and reviews—without permission of the author.

Cataloging-in-Publication Data is on file with the Library of Congress

Cover photograph by Betsey Lewis - Area 51, Nevada at sunset
Cover design by Dragonfly Dimension Design

Dragonfly Dimensions Publishing, Boise, Idaho 83709
www.dragonflydimensionspublishing.com
Contact: info@dragonflydimensionspublishing.com

Dedication

For those who have awakened from their deep winter slumber to create a beautiful new Earth. And to those who are beginning to feel the gentle stirrings of change—it's all in perfect order. There's nothing to fear as consciousness expands and elevates human DNA. The truth will burn brightly within your beautiful Spirits.

Contents

Introduction	9
Chapter One – Heaven, Hell and Angels	15
Chapter Two – Death and Dying	23
Chapter 3 – God and Reincarnation	29
Chapter 4 – Ghosts and Specters	35
Chapter 5 – Prejudice	41
Chapter 6 – UFOs, ETs, and Time Travel	45
Chapter 7 – Animal Souls	51
Chapter 8 – Walk-Ins	57
Chapter 9 – Astral Projection and Astrology	61
Chapter 10 – The New Children and Orbs	67
Chapter 11 – Miscellaneous Questions	73
Chapter 12 – The Future	81
Epilogue	99
Living Earth Wisdom	109
Bibliography	111
About the Author	113

Introduction

Since childhood I have experienced an awareness of an invisible world that coexists beside our physical reality. I can't really explain this feeling and knowing except to tell you that my entire being tells me I'm right. In my book, *Communicating with the Other Side: True Experiences of Psychic-Medium,* I wrote about my psychic experiences, precognitive warnings and communication with spirit, but in this book I felt compelled to answer more questions asked by clients, friends and family.

My first paranormal experience began at eight-months-of-age when my parents were driving on a lonely highway in Moscow, Idaho to Twin Falls in southern Idaho to visit my grandparents and other family members—which usually took eight hours. My parents left Moscow on a Friday evening, placing me in a basket on the back seat of the car. They had driven several hours and had reached New Meadows, Idaho; an area doted by farms and ranches. The odd part about the trip was the absence of cars or trucks during their drive. Suddenly a roar descended on them, sharking the car so violently they believed a plane was in distress and about to crash on them. Dad pulled to the side of the road and together they surveyed the area and sky. The roar had stopped instantly and there was no sign of a plane.

That was the story my parents had told me through the years. Then in 1980 my uncle Martin added a new mystery to their story, comparing their encounter to the famous abduction case of Betty and Barney Hill who were allegedly abducted by extraterrestrials in a rural portion of New Hampshire road on September 19, 1961 through September 20, 1961. The incident was later known as the "Hill Abduction" and the "Zeta Reticuli Incident."

Uncle Martin recalled how my parents were clearly frightened by the roar, but the strange part about their story, they couldn't account for two hours. My grandparents and everyone believed my parents were in a car accident after they failed to arrive after eight hours. I questioned my dad and mom about the missing time, but they had no recollection of it, which further complicated the story. What caused the roar? Is it possible we were all abducted that night? In many alien abduction cases abductees report missing time and erased memories of the actual event.

In 1981 and 1982 Mom and I were separately regressed by renowned MUFON (Mutual UFO Network) abduction investigator and author Ann Druffel (*The Tujunga Canyon Contacts*) in Los Angeles. The transcript of those hypnotic regression sessions can be found in my book, *Angels, Aliens and Prophecy II.* I can't tell with certainty that we had a UFO/Alien encounter that night, but I do know something strange and unnatural happened to me and my parents that night in New Meadows, Idaho.

At age three my mother said I had two invisible playmates I named Peek-a-boo and Patoy. She said I described them and they gave me messages I refused to share with my parents. My invisible friends faded from my memory by age four. Although I have no memory of my playmates, I feel they were my Spirit Guides who have guided and protected me through the years.

My next inexplicable event happened at age seven on my way home from first grade in Twin Falls, Idaho. I was chased by a giant silver disk that seemed to increase and decrease in size. Shortly after this event I was shown cataclysmic Earth changes in my dreams each night. In the dreams I watched hurricane winds the coastal areas, flash floods that came without warning, tsunami waves from ocean earthquakes, volcanoes erupting and the Earth shaking. Oddly, I was always much older in my dreams and always escaping these Earth changes with other people. I have always known the signs of an Earth in deep distress would take place later in my life, and it's all happening now as the world experiences unprecedented rains and flooding, drought, sink holes, mysterious booms, volcanoes awakening in large numbers and increased powerful earthquakes since the Nepal 7.8 magnitude earthquake April 25, 2015.

At the age of eight my beloved paternal grandfather died of a massive heart attack. This was the first death in our family, and I was so bereaved by his sudden death, I prayed nightly for a sign from him that he lived on. Late one night my prayers were answered— he appeared next to my bed as a gauzy spirit figure of a man. The experience was frightening because I didn't recognize his younger spirit form. He appeared as a slender young man and not as the overweight sixty-six year old grandfather I remembered.

Through the years I've been warned of many events, like earthquakes, Bobby Kennedy's assassination, Mount St. Helen's volcanic eruption in 1980, and 9-11. My life has been saved by invisible hands countless times, and my Spirit Guides have guided through dreams, inspirations and warned me of someone's passing. My father's voice warned me about my sister Kathy's death was closed in 2003. Shortly after Kathy's death on my father's birthday, July 19, Kathy began to make her spiritual presence known by shaking a small tree. Two years ago she decided to really make her presence known by turning off a small stereo whenever my husband and I turned on the Kool Oldies Radio station, causing kitchen utensils to levitate and messing with our large stereo and TV. Over and over things began to happen. Our cat freaked out one night, hissing and his hair on end as he stared at a photograph of Kathy in our hallway. After I explained to our cat it was Kathy's spirit he's understood that she's a welcome spirit in our home.

From 2013 to 2015 the activity always increases around the holidays, which was Kathy's favorite time of the year. Shortly after February 24, which would have been her birthday, she suddenly stopped turning off the radio. I have always prayed from my deceased relatives and friends, and I said an emotional silent prayer for Kathy to move on in the spiritual world. I wanted her to know it was fine to move on in her spiritual evolution. I had told my husband about my prayer and then on the morning of March 5, 2015, two days before my birthday, I received a surprise message from Kathy. I walked into the dining room and heard the Kool Oldies radio station playing The Jackson Five's song, ***Never Can Say Goodbye,*** and suddenly the radio switched off by itself.

My husband laughed and said, "Looks like your sister told you that she's never going to say goodbye to you. You are stuck with her!"

I'm blessed to my sister as my new Spirit Guide—they often change through our lifetime, but it looks like Kathy will be here until it's my time to pass over.

Through the years I've been given a plethora of spiritual and paranormal experiences and I want to share what I sense intuitively or have been shown by my Guides about the Other Side, about death, ghosts, UFOs, parallel dimension, reincarnation, and other questions that haunt about the unseen world around us. These are my truths, and if you find these answers ring true for you, than I've accomplished my mission in helping people realize that our world is far more incredible than what we've been told by clergy and academics. I don't ask you to believe everything I've been told, only that you consider the possibilities and keep an open mind. In some cases, the answers I've provided are from outside channeled sources.

Chapter One

Heaven, Hell and Angels

Over the course of my life I've had spirit warnings about deaths, as well as personal and global warnings. No doubt, I owe my life to my spirit guides and their patience with me. They've saved my life from two car accidents, choking, suffocating in a snow bank, drowning in a reservoir, a plane crash that should have happened, several near-fatal asthma attacks, and a group of large pine trees that should have crushed me during a camping trip in the mountains of Idaho. Other near death incidents include nearly falling from a mountain ledge, hemorrhaging from a benign tumor, and several times I tried to commit suicide as a teenager due to the turmoil in my family life.

Obviously my spirit friends have kept me around for a while longer to help others on their spiritual journey, and I'm grateful for their love and continued guidance, as I write my books and provide psychic readings for my beautiful clientele.

Through visions, my intuition, and my personal experiences and dreams, I've provided answers to what lies beyond the veiled curtain we call Death. I've also included authors who have provided more information than I have about The Other Side and other mysteries that confound us. Believe me, I don't have all the answers to life's infinitesimal mysteries, but I have a real sense of what lies beyond. So I offer my insights from my childhood Spirit Guides, Peekaboo and Patoy, my sister Kathy and my angels and hope this information will help you when someone near and dear passes on. After helping a great many people, including myself, deal with grief, I'm still amazed by the constant validations from Spirit.

The questions included here have been asked by family, friends and clientele.

The Other Side

Question: What happens when we first cross over to the Other Side?
Answer: It all depends on our individual belief systems. When we pass over we become pure energy thought forms, and we can create any scene that suits us. However, a large number of souls believe a heaven exists for the righteous and a hell exists for evil people. For those who believe this, depending on the type of person they have deemed themselves to be, they will see either a heaven or a hell. Our guides are always there to help us get reacquainted with our new surroundings again and how to us our mental powers again to create our environment.

For others who have had a long illness or died violently or tragically, they may sleep for a while, which can be months or years in Earth time. Sometimes the soul doesn't realize it has died, and spirit guides rush to their aid. Unfortunately, there are people who have died angry or full of hate, and haunt houses and buildings, using their energy in negative ways. They get trapped in a state of limbo and can't get free. The ethereal space around our planet is full of trapped, confused and angry souls and those souls need help to move on to continue on their spiritual evolution.

Greetings from the Other Side

Question: When we first pass over, who greets us on the Other Side?

Answer: It can be a departed relative or friend, and in some cases an angel or spirit guide will arrive after the soul as left the physical body or just before death takes place as a disguised family member, to ease that person into our new reality. There are stories of people who have NDEs (near-death experiences) and describe meeting Jesus, Buddha and other spiritually evolved beings. Although I can't confirm or deny their visualization of these beings, I do know that we are all met by highly evolved spiritual beings.

Remember, we are thought forms, pure energy, when we cross over, and we can create whatever we want.

Through the years I taught my sister that when she died she was pure mind and could create any reality, and be transported anywhere by her thoughts. Obviously, she learned her lesson well about the Other Side because of her many recent visits.

Spirit Guides

Question: Does everyone have a spirit guide?

Answer: Spirit guides are incorporeal beings who are assigned to you before you reincarnate into a physical body. They help nudge and guide you through life. Sometimes guides will stay through your entire life, and sometimes others replace them to help with specific life lessons. They may appear as male or female energy, but in reality they are pure energy. You are never alone. Usually guides are souls who have had physical incarnations. At times, a spirit guide will take on the appearance of a loved one who has died, to make the transition easier for the newly deceased person. From time to time more evolved beings and angels step in to help us fulfill our earthly mission.

New Souls vs Old Souls

Question: I've heard the expression "new souls." Can you elaborate on what this means?

Answer: God created all souls at the same time, but some souls have gone through the physical reincarnation progress much longer than others. Some souls have decided to visit this earthly plane for the first time and may have a hard time adjusting to the new experience. Some souls never need to go through this process of reincarnation for further evolution.

Spirit Guides and Angels

Question: Is there a difference between spirit guides and angels?

Answer: Guardian angels are highly evolved beings or energy intelligence and have never existed in a physical body since their inception. They can be called upon for any reason and have direct access to the Akashic records, the universal computer. Spirit guides assist us through life and provide insight, inspiration, and a helping hand when needed. Spirit guides are learning too, and haven't evolved as far as angels.

Heaven and Hell

Question: So if there isn't a heaven or hell, what do souls do on the Other Side?

Answer: Excellent question. Like I answered before, we create our heaven or hell. A good analogy of the Other Side is the 1998 movie, *What Dreams May Come,* starring Robin Williams, Cuba Gooding, Jr., and Annabella Sciorra.

In the story Chris Nielsen (Robin Williams) has an idyllic life with artist Annie Collins (Annabella Sciorra) and their two children. Then one day a car accident takes the life of their two beautiful children, Ian and Marie. Life becomes difficult - Annie suffers a mental breakdown and the couple contemplates divorce.

Finally they decide to reconcile, but Chris is killed in a car crash. After his death he remains earthbound and tries to communicate with Annie to help her cope with her horrible losses. When his attempts don't help Annie's deep sorrow, he moves on.

Chris awakens in Heaven and learns that what he sees there is from his own imagination. He's created his own heaven. Soon Chris meets his spiritual guide, Albert (Cuba Gooding, Jr.). Albert guides Chris in this new afterlife. He also teaches Chris about his existence in heaven, and how to shape his little corner, and to travel to others' "dreams." Meanwhile, Annie commits suicide after years of depression. She finds herself in a hellish place until Chris, in his endless love for Annie, shows her how to join him in his heaven.

Chris and Annie are reunited with their children in their heaven. At the end Chris proposes they reincarnate so he and Annie can experience life together again. The film ends with Chris and Annie meeting again as young children in a situation that parallels their first meeting.

To get back to the original question, souls can do anything on the Other Side, such as explore new worlds and the stars, watch over loved ones on Earth and take classes on any subject: the arts, music, writing, math, science, etc. Souls have a universe of options.

Evil

Question: Why is there evil?

Answer: There are worlds where evil does not exist. In our duality world evil exists for a purpose. Without evil, how would anyone learn and advance? It's a necessary balance in our world. However, the world is out of balance or *ayni* (pronounced eye-knee) as the indigenous say, and a great correction is about to happen. The Maya, the Hopi and other indigenous elders have predicted that we are going from the fourth world into the fifth world, a time when the Earth will be cleansed of negativity.

As human beings, we seek the impossible—we strive in hardships, and become better people for it. Our world is full of duality; for example, dark and light, hot and cold. Without opposites there is no growth.

Demons

Question: Do demons exist?

Answer: I have never dealt with this, but I do believe there are dark entities that reside on lower astral planes of existence. They access our world through portals, and attach themselves to people who have lowered their vibrational frequency through drugs (also allopathic prescription drugs) and excess alcohol. There are also people who attract these entities because of their misuse of the occult. There are cases where dark forces feed on the mentally ill or innocent children.

I believe our obsession with electronic gadgets, the food we eat, and some music, can lower our vibratory rate. There are negative planners who can eliminate people by lowering a person's MHz (megahertz). Some allopathic medicine, chemical prescriptions, lower the MHz of the body. Radiation from TV, cell phones and computer screens lower the MHz, and consuming processed and canned foods that have 0 MHz to support the body. Today much of our food is GMO (genetically modified), and contains corn sugar, GMO soy oil, artificial dyes, and chemicals to preserve it—you might as well be eating cardboard!

The normal vibratory rate of the human body has been determined to be between 62 and 68 MHz. The brain functions optimally between 72 and 90 MHz. When the body vibration lowers to 58 MHz, it can catch a cold; at 57 MHz the flu, 55 MHz candida, 52 MHz Epstein Barr; 42 MHz cancer, and at 25 MHz death begins.

The human body has amazing healing abilities, but the onslaught of ways to bring down the vibratory level has reached a critical point. The picture as it is at the moment is beyond discouraging. However, in playing out various scenarios in holographic possibilities is not at all impossible to reverse the outcome if humanity awakens to their enslavement.

Chapter Two

Death and Dying

Large Groups who Die Together

Question: Why do groups of people chose to die together?

Answer: All through time groups of people have exited the planet in large numbers and this is a conscious decision for all involved. Those who leave the planet in a large group, by plane crash, boating accident, natural or non-natural disaster, choose to do so for great advancement of the soul. These groups usually reincarnate together—decisions that were made on the Other Side. Those who have died trying to save others by their heroic deeds and compassion during a disaster or great tragedy will evolve the soul quickly

Suicide

Question: What happens to those who commit suicide?

Answer: Some believe suicide means eternal hell and no redemption, but they are completely wrong. Suicides do not have any particular punishment, except for the soul's choosing. However, any problems that were not faced in this life will be faced in another. There are different reasons for suicide—such as those with terminal diseases and in extreme pain, depression, mental illness, and those running from their problems, which is the hardest lesson for that soul. Escaping life's problems and taking your life is wrong and a type of suicide that the soul may spend many lifetimes resolving.

If a person kills himself believing that the act will destroy his consciousness forever, then this false idea may severely impede his soul's progress and be intensified by guilt.

Remember the soul judges self, so it is the soul's duty to either find forgiveness in self or torture self in their own created hell. As I said before, Creator, or God, does not judge us, never has and never will. Those who commit suicide to stop endless pain from a terminal illness, or accidentally die from a drug overdose, will find forgiveness faster on the Other Side than those who run from their problems and commit this act. Prayers of love and forgiveness are always needed for these souls.

In Jane Robert's channeled book on the *Seth Material* books, Jane was told by Seth that after a suicide teachers are available to explain the true situation. Various therapies are used. For example, the personality may be led back to the events prior to the decision. Then the personality is allowed to change the decision. An amnesia effect is induced, so that the suicide itself is forgotten. Only later is the individual informed of the act, when he is better able to face it and understand it. Sometimes the personality refuses to accept the face of death. The individual knows quite well that he is dead in your terms, but he refuses to complete the psychic separation. Now: There are instances of course where the individuals concerned do not realize the fact of death. It is not a matter of refusing to accept it, but a lack of perception. In this state such an individual will also be obsessed with earthly concerns, and wander perhaps bewildered throughout his home or surroundings.

Unfortunately, there are a huge number of souls trapped in this reality, and someday when humans have learned how to clear the ethereal band surrounding Earth, these lost souls will someday be released from their self-imposed prison.

Seth continued: Those who understand thoroughly that reality is self-created will have the least difficulty [on the Other Side]. Those who have learned to understand and operate in the mechanics of the dream state will have great advantage. A belief in demons is highly disadvantageous after death, as it is during physical existence. A systematized theology of opposites is also detrimental. If you believe, for example, that all good must be balanced by evil, then you bind yourself into a system of reality that is highly limiting, and that contains within it the seed of great torment.

Actor Robin Williams committed suicide inside his home by strangulation on August 11, 2014. He had suffered for years from depression, and substance abuse. It was revealed that he was diagnosed with Parkinson 's disease, a degenerative disorder of the central nervous system, which might have contributed to his suicidal thoughts.

Shortly after Robin William's death, it was reported that he began turning on the television to watch his favorite comedy shows in the house where he died. Watchmen at the California mansion are convinced his ghost is lurking there. A neighbor said: "Security goes in every couple of hours to check the alarm system but several times now the TV has been on when they've arrived."

The source said that once a stand-up show was playing starring the late Richard Pryor, who was a pal before his death in 2005. "It's typical Robin—to be playing practical jokes and making people laugh, even in the afterlife"

Even in death, Robin's spirit is still the same. My sense is that Robin wanted the world know he still has his sense of humor and he's doing just fine on the Other Side.

The Death of Infants

Question: What happens to babies and infants when they die?

Answer: These souls have chosen to leave early as a soul lesson. Sometimes the lesson involved the parents, and sometimes the infant's soul. There are no accidents in life, only lessons. Once the infant has crossed over, there are loving spirit guides to assist them until they become spiritually mature again. Some psychic believe that these are souls that committed suicide in a past life and return to make up this time to satisfy the karmic debt of suicide. I don't think this is always the case. Each soul decides what lessons they want to learn in this lifetime. Sometimes the soul realizes that the picked the wrong parents, and can't achieve certain positive experiences and soul lessons.

You say life is unfair when a baby dies, but you are wrong. Life is wonderfully fair and just. When an infant or young baby dies we cry and grieve for them, but the child does not need to be here anymore. They have already advanced, like skipping a grade in school. When a person is sick and dying, their faith is tested. How will they react and do the things needed for further spiritual advancement? Life is a never-ending school, a classroom of countless lessons.

Chapter Three

God and Reincarnation

God

Question: Are we judged by God on the Other Side?

Answer: No. God, or Creator, does not judge souls. You judge yourself for the positive and negative things you've done in the span of your life. Many people who have NDEs (near-death experiences) tell that they had a life review, like a movie, of everything done in a lifetime. You experience it all. This can be quite painful, but it serves to help the soul evolve and prepare for the next incarnation.

Shirley MacLaine's book, *What If*

Question: Hollywood actress Shirley MacLaine suggested in her new book, *What If,* that six million Jews and millions of others systematically murdered in Hitler's death camps in World War II were balancing their karma for crimes committed in past lives and that cosmologist Professor Stephen Hawking may have subconsciously given himself his debilitating motor neurone disease of ALS. How do you feel about this?

Answer: Shirley has always had a way of pushing buttons with her metaphysical, new age beliefs. I totally disagree with her when it comes to karma. Souls can take on great hardships, disasters, and disabilities to evolve much faster as spiritual beings. It is their choice. In some cases when a person murders another, the victim and the murderer have a specific karmic tie with each other from a past life. If a murder is committed, there is always karma, either instant or in another lifetime. There is no escaping the cosmic *Law of Cause and Effect*. Other times there is no karmic link, but each soul must work out their individual karma from past lives. Stephen Hawking may have decided that experiencing such a debilitating disease would help him advance on the spiritual ladder, and I'd say it has worked. He has overcome great obstacles and helped many people with ALS who would have given up without someone like Hawking to inspire them.

Karma is growth and evolution.

How Fast Do We Reincarnate?

Question: I read somewhere that a soul can reincarnate every 18 minutes. Is this true, and how does the soul find the right parents? What if they have reincarnated already?

Answer: There are currently over seven billion human souls on Earth, and I'm sure they are returning faster than every 18 minutes. It is estimated that 134 million babies are born per year. How soon a soul reincarnates it entirely up to them. There is always a choice, but some souls are very impatient and decided to reincarnate immediately after death. There are countless stories of souls who reincarnated soon after death, especially in third world countries like Tibet and India. This is usually a bad idea because the soul needs more time to evaluate its previous life before taking on a new earthly body. From what I've learned, most souls reincarnate within one hundred years, which gives them time to access their Akashic soul records. Spirit guides are there to assist the newly arrived soul plan for the next adventure.

As far as finding the right parents, that's a mutual agreement between you and your soul friends. Your mother might decide to return as your sister in the next incarnation, or your father might be an uncle, or your brother might become your child. Most souls like to stay together and work on spiritual lessons together. There are some souls who want to seek new relationships, and that's perfectly fine too.

Not all growth happens in one lifetime, or in this earthy plane; it can be done on the Other Side without a physical body. But soul growth is so much faster in the physical realm, and the tests and lessons much harder. Reincarnation is real, and allows the soul to manifest itself again in this physical world, or in other worlds, in order to evolve.

Past Lives and The Present

Question: Are past lives relevant to this life?

Answer: Absolutely! On occasion, healing and lessons need to take place from events that happened in past lives. Dr. Brian Weiss, an American psychiatrist and New York bestselling author, was astonished and skeptical when one of his patients began recalling past-life traumas that seemed to hold the key to her recurring nightmares and anxiety attacks. His skepticism was eroded, however, when she began to channel messages from "the space between lives," which contained remarkable revelations about Dr. Weiss's family and his dead son. Using past-life therapy, he was able to cure the patient and embark on a new, more meaningful phase of his own career.

Dr. Brian Weiss first book was, *Many Lives, Many Master,* an excellent book on reincarnation followed by six more books on the subject. I highly recommend his books.

Reincarnation

Question: Why must we reincarnate?

Answer: You were given free-will. If you decide you've had enough of Earth, you do not need to return. Your spirit guides help you assess your spiritual growth and your options.

The universe is never ending and expanding. We are the same: never ending, playing out different roles and dramas, learning, growing, evolving and transforming, like caterpillars that change into beautiful butterflies.

Remembering Past Lives

Question: If reincarnation really exists, why don't I recall these past lives?

Answer: Can you imagine your brain holding hundreds even thousands of lifetime memories—of lost loves, children, parents, pain, births, and perhaps even tragic and painful deaths? It would cause insanity or certainly mess with you mentally and emotionally. Don't we have a difficult enough time living from day to day in our present reality?

Some children recall past lives until they reach the ages of seven or eight years old and then the past life memories slowly fade.

Many people get hints of past lives by the type of music they like, the people they instantly like or dislike, the food they eat, the places they like to visit or hope to visit, unexplained phobias, hobbies like collecting antiquities from a certain era like Civil War guns. Even our dreams can provide hints to past lives. I recalled a past life in a dream of ancient catacombs somewhere in the Holy land, but that's all I remember. I've also experienced glimpses of a past lives in the old West and ancient Egypt.

My mother recalled a past life as a Chinese laborer who worked on the Great Wall of China and died and was buried inside the Great Wall, an unknown fact when she was a child growing up in the 1930s.

Who determines if we will be born male or female?

Question: Who determines if we are born male or female in each lifetime?

Answer: It depends on what is needed for our soul growth. Our guides and council help us select the roles we will take in the new incarnations. The major reason we return is for soul growth and to learn unconditional love. Because we are able to forget who we were in the past, this makes it so much easier to learn things on a deeper level and expand even more from it. If humanity learned that we were created by the same God force, there would be more tolerance, more love, and more compassion for one another. We would see the divine spark in all living creatures and honor that spark. Most souls decide on the same sex they were in a prior lifetime.

Soul Mates

Question: Do soul mates exist?

Answer: I prefer "soul friends." We have many soul friends who travel with us in life times for the adventure and spiritual lessons. A soul mate doesn't have to be a husband, or wife, not a sexual relationship. A soul mate can be a sister, friend, brother, neighbor, or even a stranger who helps you along your path. A soul mate is someone you've known in prior lifetimes and who helps you work out karma in this lifetime. A soul mate for eternity is a romantic thought but not a practical one—but don't despair because most of our soul mates are with us lifetime after lifetime. We are like actors on a stage, creating each exciting experience for soul growth. Every soul has the ability to decide on the type of experience they want to play out. It's all a wonderful God-given adventure.

Chapter Four

Ghosts and Specters

People Who Pass Angry or an Abusive Parent

Question: Suppose I had an argument with my mother or father before they died. Will they carry their anger to the Other Side? What about an abusive parent?

Answer: Never will a good person who has passed hold anger in their heart for petty arguments and disagreements. Death doesn't change a person's character or personality. However, there are souls who have carried deep resentment and hate in their hearts because of injustices and untimely deaths, which keeps them earthbound and reliving the past. These malevolent ghosts haunt houses and produce a lot of negative energy at those who enter their world. Until these sad souls learn to release their hate and anger they will be trapped in an endless limbo world. Only love and forgiveness will release them from their eternal hell.

Ghosts and Specters

Questions: Can you tell me more about ghosts or specters?

Answer: Most often a soul doesn't realize they have died and keep repeating the events that lead to their death, a kind of loop in space. Sometimes a soul doesn't believe in anything beyond the physical world, and they get trapped in their own limbo world—a world of their creation. Prayers can help them to get back into the flow of everlasting life again. Unfortunately, there are souls who refuse to enter the light and evolve, and it might take hundreds, and maybe even thousands of Earth years for them to realize their mistake.

There are some souls that are trapped on the Earth plane by a negative force or forces that prevent them from moving forward into the higher spiritual realm. A positive mind propels us forward, and negative ones set us back. As I stated earlier, these sick minds can be healed by those in the spiritual realm or by human prayers.

People have seen ghosts, gauzy apparitions, mists and other shadows and whitish images. Once someone passes their vibration rate increases, but their energy and personality essence still survives physical death. What we are seeing is their energy essence and those who have practiced can materialize this ectoplasmic image. Emotion helps to create a stronger image when people have passed in a violent way, angry way or unexpected way. There are theories that when a spirit actually lows down their vibration the human eye can capture it, but most of the time they are vibrating in a parallel world next to our physical world.

Contacting the Deceased

Question: How long does it take for my deceased loved one to contact me?

Answer: Time, as we know it here on Earth, doesn't exist to them. Our loved ones hear our thoughts and prayers, which pull them to us instantly. They are around us all the time. Often their signs and messages are dismissed because most people don't want to believe that spirits can communicate with us from the spirit world. It may take years before you are aware or open to their validations. Sometimes it happens within moments of their passing, or it may take hours, days or even years. There are no set rules.

There are well-known mediums that make it seem like spirits can be summoned on demand, but this is not true! It seems more likely that the medium is reading someone's thoughts about their deceased loved one than actually getting spirit information.

I'm sure your next question is how do I know if I've received validation of their existence on the Other Side? Well, it's those things you call coincidences, but they aren't coincidences. Do you hear their favorite song played whenever you turn on the radio? Do you hear your name whispered before you wake up in the morning? Do you smell their favorite scent or perfume? Did you have a vivid dream where they spoke to you, and that dream seemed real? Did you feel someone stroking your face with a feather-like touch? Doe butterflies or dragonflies hover over you? Did a seeming miracle take place in your life, and you can't explain how it happened? Did an inspiration pop into your head out-of-the-blue one morning or did you receive a warning that saved your life?

Did you know that countless songwriters, authors, and inventors claim their invention, song or and inspiration came to them in a dream or a sudden inspiration. These are all validations from spirit of their eternal love and guidance.

One other thing I'd like to mention: through the centuries people have contacted the Other Side through Ouija boards, automatic writing and séances. If you don't know what you are doing you can conjure up dark entities who like to entice you into a game of control. They can enter into your body if you are not protected in the Light—and this is possession. People who indulged in heavy drugs and alcohol invite these entities into them. Once in my lifetime I met someone I believed was possessed each time he drank heavily. His facial features changes and his eyes became malevolent and evil. He was extremely violent during these episodes.

How do I communicate with the Other Side?

Question: What is the best way to start communication with the Other Side?

Answer: What is your motive? Do you want to know that a loved one is doing all right or do you want answers to your life? My sister Kathy, my father, my mother and various spirits have contacted me through the years and made it clear they are real. I honor their space and so I suggest to you to do the same. Pray for them and ask for a sign. If you are demanding they contact you, I doubt if you will get any kind of confirmation. Remember they are only a vibration away, and hear our thoughts and our prayers. Believing is the first step. Most of us have preconceived ideas that the dead can communicate—and they'd be dead wrong. They are more alive than we are on this plane of existence.

Seat in mediation each day at a specific time and ask that you receive a sign, and then be patient. Be open to signs and messages—lights flickering, radio turning off, you loved ones scent, a dragonfly or butterfly that hovers over your head or lands on you out of the clear blue, a bird that keep returning to visit. Allow heightened consciousness and awareness of your surroundings and everything that is happening around you—open your heart and mind to infinite possibilities. For some this might take practice and patience.

Animal Communication

Question: How can I communicate with my pets?

Answer: Send them images, which they understand. They will also send you images. Understand their body language. Animals do talk in their own way. A few years ago I attended a spiritual conference in Santa Fe, New Mexico, and my husband stayed home to care for our dog Oreo and cat Comet. Each day he reported how they were acting up and really upset about my absence. On the day I planned to return home, I began sending them telepathic messages that I'd return that day, and I asked my husband to let them know. He said it was like magic—both Oreo and Comet began to act normal. I have no doubt they completely understood.

There are excellent classes in animal communication in the United States and in other countries.

Chapter Five

Prejudice

There is so much prejudice in our world with regards to religion, sexual preference, color of skin, politics. Internet forums have become a place where people, groups, and kids can hide behind fictitious names and berate others. I have no doubt that these people would never say these cruel and thoughtless things to someone's face, yet they feel free to do so on the internet because no one knows there true identity. In the Bible it says, "Judge not least ye be judged." This is the cosmic boomerang that will come back to anyone who judges others by their malicious words or actions. Sadly, young people have been driven to commit suicide by such cruelty.

Homosexuality

Question: It seems there is more homosexuality in the world than ever before? Does God condemn this act?

Answer: I will say this to you again—God never judges us and has created all souls equally. Actually, the soul is neither male nor female, nor any color. It is sad that people hold up the Bible and say it says this or that, but these are not God's words, they are man's words.

Remember Matthew 7:1, "Judge not least ye be judged." What it means that we will be judged when we judge others—this is the way of karma.

These souls might have incarnated too quickly and that past life as a male or female still is fresh in their subconscious. A great number of homosexuals are coming into the planet with a message for all of humanity—that the human soul is neither male nor female. It is a big lesson for all at this time to accept each other, and look beyond race, religion, and sexual preference.

We are all God's children and have a right to be here to learn lessons of love. When we despise someone we despise God, because we are made from his mind.

In the beautiful book, *Kiss of God: The Wisdom of A Silent Child,* Marshall Stewart Ball, a brilliant child who was born with severe disabilities and unable to speak or walk, stunned his parents with his ability to understand life and the concept of God. Since the age of six he had completed hundreds of pages of writings. Marshall wrote in 1994, at age seven, "To judge another is to Judge God."

Although Marshall was never told about reincarnation, at age eight, he wrote, "Marshall has been here for millions of lifetimes."

Marshall is one of the new children, here to reteach us the art of love, compassion and understanding. As Marshall wrote, "Perfect love kindly will give each thought special direction," and "Answers come to good listeners that hear God. Go to God and God will teach you."

Creator's love is so great for all souls, it's all encompassing. Everyone is beautiful in God's eyes.

Why do humans hate others because of their skin color, their religion, and their sexual preference? In the spiritual realm none of this exists, and there is no reason to hate, yet on the earthly plane we find endless reasons to judge and hate each other. It's senseless.

It's time we see the divine light in all God's creations.

Chapter Six

UFO, ETs and Time Travel

Extraterrestrials

Question: There are stories of extraterrestrials seen with departed relatives. Do they access this reality?

Answer: Excellent question and a hard one to answer. From what I've sensed there are endless dimensions and worlds that co-exist with Earth. Parallel dimensions are being explored by scientists in the world of quantum physics.

Question: Is it true that the Other Side could be accessed by a variety of beings?

Answer: I believed it is possible. Everything is vibration, and there are many beings who are highly evolved, both spiritually and intellectually, that can move through time portals and space. I've always felt we are watched all the time by unseen beings, and everything we do and say is known and recorded.

When it comes to quantum physics and the unseen world, time travel comes into play. Theoretical scientists believe time as we know it does to exist. The past, present and future are all happening at once, but on different planes of existence. Many times we get glimpses of a probable future with a vision or premonition, but that probably future can be changes. Does time travel exist? I have no doubt, and that many of the beings visiting us are from other time lines and dimensions.

We are babies just beginning to learn what the universe is made of and all its extraordinary mysteries.

Time Travel

Question: Is there time travel, and can we manipulate time?
Answer: Early I discussed time travel, but will go into it further. Quantum physicists believe time travel is possible. There have been many experiments, such as the double-slit experiment, or Young's experiment, where electrons and protons were fired into a panel with two slits. What appeared on the panel were three smudges, which baffled the scientists. Something strange and unknown was taking place.

There are stories of time travel and time slips where people from this time period suddenly find themselves propelled in another era, usually from the past. Perhaps this could explain the mysterious disappearances of people, ships, planes and boats.

Time is a construct. All time is simultaneous. A planet has layers of energy grids around it that allow it to be experienced from its various time frames. Earth has many portals where beings can enter into our reality.

Some of these time portals exist in the Mexico/Central America area, California's Mount Shasta, the Mideast, Easter Island, Mount Fuji, Lake Titicaca, the Nazca lines in Peru, Uluru (or Ayers) Rock in Australia, and the Bermuda Triangle. There is also one in the Sinai, and there is one over Tibet. These are some of the major portals through which energies arrive and depart on our planet.

There are those highly evolved people on Earth, like Tibetan monks, who can access these portals and peer into the future. This is how they prepared for the invasion of Tibet by the Chinese. They took valuable artifacts and ancient texts to be hidden as they fled Tibet for India to go into exile. This is how His Holiness The Dalai Lama survived the invasion of Tibet. The Tibetan Oracle had foreseen the invasion of Tibet by the Chinese long before it happened.

Time lines can be changed by creating a Prime Event, such as the Harmonic Convergence in 1987, organized by Dr. Jose Arguelles. Millions of people heard about this event and gathered in meditation and prayer on August 16-17, 1987. Through their prayers the Berlin Wall eventually came down in 1989.

Another time line change happened on 9-11 in 2001. Our world was altered on that day. In order to anchor a new time line onto the planet, there has to be a mass event that takes place.

The Harmonic Convergence was created from a future time line and set into the present. What created this event?—the mass consciousness of people, uniting in love and peace.

I truly believe and have been told by spirit that we can change events and time lines when humanity unites in a common benevolent goal. We are the masters of our fate, and the sooner we awaken to this fact, the sooner our planet will be healed, and peace will envelop the world.

UFO Encounters

Question: You have written about your UFO experiences and perhaps an alien encounter in your book, *Angels, Aliens and Prophecy II,* but can you tell me why are they here?

Answer: Since childhood I've known that life is everywhere, and that intelligence beings watch us. I believe we are about to awaken *en masse* to other realities and dimensional beings soon. I believe they are here to help us on our evolutionary path. There are many species of beings watching us, and like humans, some of them are highly evolved spiritually, and others aren't and have less than positive agenda for humanity.

I recently had the opportunity to interview Ron Felber about his book *Searchers: The True Story of Alien Abduction,* based on the true account of a young couple, Steve and Dawn, from Southern California, who were held hostage in 1989 by alien beings for twelve hours in the Mojave Desert of California.

This is one of the most believable alien abductions I've ever read. Steve and Dawn agreed to hypnosis to uncover more of their alien abduction story, and this is what they revealed:

"The aliens want to make contact with us. They were sent on missions throughout the universe by the One Supreme."

A question asked of Dawn: "You talked about the universe and matter earlier. You said, 'Our universe ends where theirs begins…'"

Dawn answered, "Our universe ends when its matter stops mattering to us and starts mattering to them." Dawn also said these beings would intervene into our world if war or mass destruction seemed imminent.

When asked what the One Supreme asks of us, the reply was, "For all the galaxies to live harmoniously together."

And so I leave you to contemplate that grand concept!

Chapter Seven

Animal Souls

Animal Souls

Question: I've heard that animals don't have souls. Can you clarify this for me?

Answer: Yes, animals most definitely do have souls, and are sentient beings. They also reincarnate. Animals are brilliant, and in many ways much smarter than humans. Animals are connected to both the physical and spiritual world and sense when someone or something is going to die or when a disaster is near. Animals know they don't end when they die. Animals move through dimensions.

Animals are more concerned with their surroundings than humans, and can move from one dimension to the next. Also, every living creature dreams, just like humans. They are creating the world they live in, just as humans create the world we exist in today.

Animals are here to teach us valuable lessons, and to hold the vibrational rate of the planet. They hold the vibrational rate of the Earth through their songs, toning and energies.

Realize that there is great intelligence in all life forms. As we open ourselves to new energies that flow through all life, we open ourselves to a deeper form of Earth relationship. All creatures hold the vibrational rate of Mother Earth, and without them we wouldn't survive.

Many people abuse animals while thinking that their harm does not matter. Any harm or abuse to animals on the planet, anywhere, is recorded on the Akashic Records. All that Creator has created is not to be taken lightly, from the lowest to the highest of animals.

Have you noticed that cats and dogs have individual personalities, just like humans, and that they demonstrate reasoning and intelligence? Have you noticed that your pet is intuitive, knows time, and can read your thoughts? Have you also noticed that they dream, feel emotion, and feel pain? There are stories of heroic animals—dogs, cats and even feral animals and sea creatures that have saved human lives. They are sentient beings to be honored and respected.

How could God's creatures not have souls? Animals don't evolve in the same way as humans, but they do evolve and grow. Everything evolves and returns to the God consciousness.

I'll relate my own personal story. I once had a beautiful black and tan hound dog puppy, named Halley. She was so amazing and so smart, but one day she seemed lethargic and sickly.

That night an angelic being appeared in my dream and said, "I must take your dog soon. It's her time to go." I pleaded for the angel to spare my beloved dog, but the angelic woman only smiled and said, "She will be fine."

Days later our veterinarian discovered Halley had a fox tail, a barbed weed, embedded deep within her body, which had traveled to her spine. She stopped eating as her hind legs became paralyzed. There was nothing more that could be done except put Halley down. The dream told me that animals do cross over into the spirit world with us, and have their own angels and spirit guides. They reincarnate to be with us from lifetime to lifetime.

One of the most amazing videos of animal communication with a black leopard appeared on YouTube. Animal whisper/communicator Anna Breytenbach, of South Africa, has dedicated her life to what she calls 'interspecies communication'. In a video documentary Anna transformed an angry black leopard named Diablo into a relaxed, contented cat.

When Anna arrived at the Jukani Wildlife Sanctuary in South Africa, she was given little information about the angry black leopard. She looked directly into the big cat's eyes, and said that he was awed by his surroundings but stressed by the treatment he received at his prior residence (a zoo). Anna sensed that the animal had been abused and had become wary of humans. He also disliked the dark name Diablo, and asked that his name be changed.

Anna said the big cat commanded respect. He was powerful both physically and in wisdom. Diablo was renamed Spirit, and soon began to explore his new surroundings outside his cage. He became a different cat. This video is proof that animals have great intelligence and wisdom, if we'd only take time to honor them.

To learn more about Anna and her amazing work, visit her website at: www.animalspirit.org

Dolphins and Whales

Question: Scientists say that dolphins and whales are more intelligent than humans, but what have these animals done for the world?

Answer: Whales and dolphins tone, creating vibrational sounds that hold our world together. They play a vital part in the planet. As I said earlier, without these highly evolved sea creatures and other creatures, including insects, our world would not exist. To destroy them would be to destroy our world because they hold our energy grid together.

We can learn to dream with them, and create a new Earth. They are waiting for us to learn this potent lesson, and to heal the planet.

Vegetarianism

Question: There continues to be a debate about vegetarian's verses meat eaters, but who is right?

Answer: Both! Ancient man/woman depended on meat to survive. Indigenous people and ancient people honored the wild food they killed, and realized the godliness in all creatures, so the animal was thanked and blessed for the food it provided. Native American tribes have ceremonies to honor an animal killed for food or a tree cut down for their Sun Dance ceremony. Nothing is taken for granted. Today most cattle, pigs, sheep, and chickens are abused, as videos and news reports indicate. They are fed food, mostly GMO corn, that they would never eat normally, and some are given hormones to fatten them up before the slaughter.

Animals sense their death, releasing the fear hormone in their bodies before they are slaughtered. The consumer then eats the meat containing the fear hormone as well as other toxic substances fed to them. Is it any wonder that humans have so many health problems and cancers from the toxic food we eat?

If the body feels good living on a vegetarian diet, this is great. Others, though, might need some meats, and that's fine too. However, too much red meat is bad for any system, because of the high iron content. If you must eat meat, find animals that are free range, grass fed and treated well.

All creatures that are eaten should be honored for providing food, including fish the way our ancestor and indigenous people have for thousands of years. Anything killed was prayed over and thank for its life. But now creatures are being killed *en masse*, rounded up and slaughtered without any compassion or remorse, like the wild horses in Nevada and dolphins in Japan. Humans must again learn to live in balance with Mother Earth, a living being, and walk in a sacred way upon her. All creatures are sentient beings with intelligence, souls, and they help hold the Earth's grid together by their travels into other realms. They are constantly traveling to other realities and anchoring the grid through their sounds and toning. Without them, life on earth would not exist. Everything is connected to spirit and has a reason for being here.

Chapter Eight

Walk-Ins

Walk-Ins

Question: In 1984 Ruth Montgomery channeled the book, *Strangers Among Us,* about walk-ins. Do they really exist?

Answer: Yes, and I've met two "walk-ins" through the years. Both of them said one day they woke up and felt their families weren't their families anymore. Their families had become strangers overnight. Nothing seemed right to them. They no longer had the same interests, and no longer shared a connection with families, spouses or friends.

I sense the walk-in phenomenon isn't happening as much now. According to Ruth Montgomery, earthly souls make an agreement with a soul on the Other Side to switch places. This is a mutual agreement between two souls. Walking into an adult body provides the vehicle to complete the soul's mission much faster than incarnating as a baby and going through years to be an adult to accomplish their soul mission.

This is not a spirit possession but a love agreement.

Telekinesis

Question: You've mentioned on talk radio shows that you can cause lights to go out and affect electricity. Can you give some examples of this?

Answer: Since childhood I've had the ability to cause street lights to go off, as well as rows of ceiling lights at grocery stores and department stores, which my husband can attest to. I don't consciously will the lights to go out, but somehow they do.

During my teen years I conducted an experiment with the fifties Studebaker I wrote about earlier in the book. It was late at night as I drove home on a country road, alone, and decided to steer the car with my thoughts. Remember, this car didn't have power steering, making it difficult to control.

I felt an immense power take over, steering the Studebaker while it remained on the road, without drifting to either side of the highway. This lasted for several minutes until I felt a presence in the back seat and lost control of the car, nearly going into a ditch.

I haven't tried the experiment again. I have learned through the years that I can will things to happen, but I never attempt to control people against their will. I learned that lesson as a child.

Recently my husband, Rick, and I were shopping at Costco. He stood a few feet from me as I pondered over which cheese to purchase. He heard a pop directly above me as one light went out, followed by an entire row of lights. I was oblivious to what had just happened, but suspected something when Rick shook his head and started laughing. This happens all the time, and I'm sure someday I'll be banned from shopping at those stores.

Not long ago I conducted a little survey on Facebook. At least ten people responded with stories of how they can make street lights to go out as they walk under them. There must be thousands of us with this psi ability. Just think what we could accomplish if we put our minds to it. That's a whole lot of energy to tap into!

Chapter Nine

Astral Projection and Astrology

Astral Projection

Question: Is it true that we all astral project into other worlds when we dream, and even see our loved ones who have passed on?

Answer: When we dream our subconscious mind leaves the physical body and is free to roam in the astral world. In a sense, each night that you sleep you enter the death world. When you wake from dream and sense it was real, it was. What do the ancient Hindus, medieval civilizations, countless modern-day scientists and spiritual leaders have in common?

They've all extensively documented the theory of astral travel, or **out-of-body experiences** (OBEs)—the theory that it's possible for a person to leave the physical body, and experience something BEYOND the physical realm. **The Dalai Lama** has said that "consciousness can be trained to leave the physical body". Studies have suggested that **up to 5% of Americans have experienced some form of astral travel.** And scientific journals have documented experiments where participants **can be induced into an out of body experience.**

I had one conscious OBE when I was sixteen and it was totally unexpected and lasted only second as I hovered above my body. My mother had the ability to be in two places at once and friends and family often remarked how she was in Idaho and at the same time in Southern California. She had an amazing psychic talent.

Astrology

Question: Is my life destined by the stars?

Answer: Before you came into this reality, you applied for a slice of time, the moment you were born. At the exact time of your birth, the stars, planets, sun, and moon were in a specific configuration. When you emerged from your mother's womb, the energy from the stars and planets were imprinted on your physical form, no matter where you were born, because the energy was touching Earth at that time. Within that time you were assigned certain probabilities, specific opportunities, certain gifts and talents and soul lessons. You decided on your parents, your lineage, a bloodline that you were born into, to give you opportunities that you felt would be ideal for you to experience in this lifetime. You determined these experiences before your birth based on what you had created in prior lifetimes, what you will create, and are creating in other places and timelines.

You have been told that astrology is meaningless, but we already know that the moon, sun, and planets all have an electromagnetic pull on our world and all life. You were given free will and the stars provide a road map for your life, given the opportunities you agreed on before your birth.

Do you believe that you only create your reality in certain areas of your life and that in other areas you are disempowered? Do you believe you have no control over most areas of your life and that the negative things in your life just happened? Do you give up easily and believe you have no control over your life? We all create the events in our life, both positive and negative. Thoughts are pure energy—so where do you think that energy goes?

It's a hard concept for us to grasp but we are responsible for our lives, even babies that die young or children abused and starving. Whenever we buy into the victim mentality, you send people the idea that they are powerless and you make that probability one for yourselves. You must learn to honor other people's dramas and lessons, knowing they made the choice to go through this before incarnation into their physical body. You must understand that others must go through the realms of physical density to bring them to light. Sometimes the greatest enlightenment happens in the greatest catastrophes and the greatest difficulties.

It's all right to assist others, but to a point. If that person is not changing their life, you have done enough and you must set them free to work out their own lessons.

Life is like a restaurant where you can order what you want. Manifestation in the physical world sometimes takes a little longer than the spiritual realm, but you must visualize what you want and be patient. Have you ever noticed that certain celebrities were told early in their career that they would never amount to anything? They didn't buy it! Instead they worked hard to achieve success and never believed the doubters.

Thought creates experience. Think of yourself as a divine, magnificent and powerful being. Eliminate the words *should* and *trying* from your vocabulary and replace them with *can, did, "I am doing," "I am manifesting,"* and *"I am intending."*

When you become a doer and you are able to create what you want in life, you set an example for others. When you believe that there is a limited amount of everything, you put restrictions on your belief system and make it a reality. When you begin to show that you can bend the laws of time and space, others will follow you. There is no limitation on anything! Whenever gifts of spirit and materiality come your way, don't think that you are luckier than others. Simply understand you know who the universe works and have applied those principles.

Most of us grew up with the belief given to us by our parents that we had to work hard to achieve anything in life. We were told what our parents were told and it's been handed down from generation to generation. Manifestation is our birth right. Do the impossible—you can do it, and together we can transform our world no matter what state the world is in—it's called mass consciousness

Chapter Ten

The New Children and Orbs

The New Children

Question: There are books on the Crystalline, Indigo, New Children, Star Children, and Rainbow Children born in the last fifteen years. Who are these children and why have they arrived?

Answer: In the last twenty plus years a large number of children have come into the world with special gifts and talents that are beyond normal. They are supernatural children, who remember where they existed before birth and recall past lives. They see and communicate with spirits; they possess telepathic, telekinetic and psychic gifts as well innate talents that make them prodigies in healing, the arts, science, mathematics, music, and writing.

Doctors often mislabel the new children as autistic, ADD, ADHD, or suggest other behavioral difficulties, but what they don't understand is these children are vibrating on a higher frequency, with changed DNA.

More than half the time, these doctors are wrong. The new children are not defective. Unfortunately, many of these children have gone unnoticed and appreciated by the world. Some of these special children have made themselves known by changing the world through creating charities that stop starvation in third world countries and help build schools for their education. One such charity is Free the Children at www.freethechildren.com. The charity began in 1995 when Craig Kielburger gathered 11 school friends to begin fighting child labor. He was 12.

I have met many of the new children, and know they have arrived to change the world through their higher vibrations. They offer us hope for an improved world. Suggested books: *The Children of Now* by Meg Blackburn Losey, Ph.D. and *The Indigo Children* by Lee Carroll.

For seniors in the world, you are the Golden Indigos born during the 40s, 50s, and 60s who paved the way for the evolved new children that began coming in to the Earth's plane during the 1980s.

Recently I was stunned by 26-year-old rapper Prince Eu's YouTube video titled, *Dear Future Generation, Sorry.* Obviously this young man remembers why he came into this earthly plane to help heal Mother Earth. I hope you will take the time to watch this amazing video and know that each of us can make a difference in the world. Please share this video with everyone you know. Thank you!

Orbs

Question: Lately I've seen orb photographs posted everywhere on the internet. What are they?

Answer: Orbs are pure intelligence. I have photographed them, and I have a friend who captured remarkable orb photographs in the Redwood trees in Northern California. The orbs actually produced streaks marks across the photograph, which meant they moved from photograph to photograph. I have another friend Diane who lives in upper New York State and she is constantly capturing strange and beautiful orbs, both at night and during the day. She has a connection to these beings.

Not all orb photographs are intelligent beings—ghosts, dimensional beings or extraterrestrials. Orbs can be bits of airborne dust, water droplets, insects etc. caught in the flash of a camera. They appear out of focus because they are so close to the lens of the camera in an area called 'The orb zone' which is between the camera lens and the point of focus in a photograph (namely the object you are taking a photo of, such as a person.)

When the flash of a camera goes off it will reflect off of the airborne object in 'the orb zone' and the position between the lens and the 'point of focus' will cause the light reflection to appear as a circle of confusion. I've photographed snow falling where orbs appear on the photographs. This was caused by the camera's flash reflecting off the snowflakes—nothing paranormal.

Orbs have been seen where crop circles are formed, where they have been seen in the sky, and the three children of Fatima, Portugal, in 1917, watched an orb float in from the east, and materialize into a Marian apparition. Orbs have also been photographed in cemeteries. Ghostly orbs are caught on camera by ghost hunters for various TV shows, and can be quite photogenic when they want to be. Even TLC's Long island Medium Theresa Caputo featured a client who captured an orb on her cell phone as it bounced around her house. Theresa sensed it was the woman's deceased child.

One of the more interesting accounts of orbs is in Dr. Meg Blackburn Losey's book, *The Children of Now,* where Dr. Losey described living children who have connected with her in orb form. At first she thought it was her imagination, but she has learned that the phenomenon is real. She wrote that she found a group of children who communicate telepathically, and there is a small group she calls the "Beautiful Silent Ones." They are the amazing children who, at a glance, appear to be considerably less than perfect, in fact nonfunctional, with severe disabilities, at least on the outside. Many have autism. They are the Crystalline, or Children of the Stars, but they are most definitely here with evolutionary energetic patterns.

Dr. Losey believes these children are the forerunners of the new evolution of humanity—they are the thousands of "new" children arriving now.

Orbs can be intelligence in many forms, here to awaken our consciousness. They are deceased souls, celestial beings, dimensional beings, angels, and living children, but they can also be explained as water, insects and other explainable on the camera lens.

Chapter Eleven

Miscellaneous Questions

Spirit Saving Lives

Question: I've heard stories of how spirits have saved lives? Can you relate any story about that?

Answer: Here's a miracle story that happened recently. Jennifer Grosbeck, a 25-year-old mother was returning home with her 18-month-old baby, Lily, after visiting her parents on March 6. Something caused Jennifer's car to go off the side of the road and plunge in the river near Spanish Fork, Utah. The car was turned upside down in the river. Fourteen hours later a fisherman happened to be in the area and spotted the hidden car under the bridge and called authorities. Four police officers arrived at the scene and heard a distinct female voice from the car saying, "help me, help us," and that is when we said, "We're trying to help you. We're trying our best to get you out."

The voice was clear as day," said Spanish Fork police officer Tyler Beddoes. That mysterious female voice increased the policemen's adrenaline which enabled them to pull the heavy, water-logged car onto its side. That's when they found the mother dead at the wheel, but her 18-month-old baby was still miraculously alive strapped her infant seat upside down. Lily had somehow survived 14 hours, in temperatures that dipped to as low as 20 degrees Fahrenheit.

What makes this story so incredible is the mother died on impact, so how did they police officers hear a voice? Was it the mother or spiritual guides/angels? Knowing how a mother's instinct is to save her child, I have no doubt that Jennifer was there with her daughter all night. Not even death could stop Jennifer from saving her baby.

All seven emergency responders had to be hospitalized and treated for hypothermia after being in the very cold river, yet Lily survived 14 hours in the cold. Although in critical condition, she has now been released from the hospital and is doing very well with her father. I'd say Lily has an important mission in this world.

Spirits on Talk Shows

Question: Have you ever had spirit come through during a talk show interview?

Answer: Several times, but in 2013 I was invited on BTR talk radio show with host Java Bob. Before the show he mentioned his young daughter had passed away the year before. In fact, it was the anniversary of her passing the night of my interview. During the interview I kept hearing a small child's voice whisper repeatedly, "Babba Jav! Babba Jav!" The voice was persistent, yet playful.

I couldn't get the voice out of my head through the entire interview and knew a child had a message for Bob. Finally I felt compelled to say something on air. "Did your daughter have a funny pet name for you, like Babba Jav?"

There was a long silence and then he laughed, "She did, in fact, call me Babba Jav. How incredible you picked that up tonight." I was honored to have validated his daughter's love from the Other Side.

I don't believe spirits can be commanded to communicate any time, any place. They show up when there is something important or urgent to convey to a loved one. We all need our space, and it should be this way with spirits—we should honor their space.

Best Selling Author William Peter Blatty

Question: Your step uncle William Peter Blatty, author of *The Exorcist,* has written books on his own paranormal experiences in a new book, *Finding Peter.* His new book is about the strange events that have taken place since the sudden death of his 19-year-old son Peter. Can you tell us more about his supernatural experiences?

Answer: I need to digress here and explain how William Peter Blatty became my step uncle. In 1971 my mom met Bill Blatty's older brother Maurice Blatty through a Beverly Hills dating agency and a few months later they were married in Las Vegas. This was shortly after *The Exorcist* was published and became a New York bestselling novel.

In Bill Blatty's 1973 autobiography, *I'll Tell Them I Remember You,* he revealed how the supernatural had influenced his life and his belief in life after death, especially after his mother's passing when he witnessed a phone lift from the cradle by itself and other objects levitate by themselves. One night he witnessed a UFO. I was given the opportunity to ask him about UFOs when he lived in Malibu, and he said he has seen some strange things hovering over the ocean at night. He wondered if he was seeing military operations from Vanderberg Air Force Base.

In an effort to make contact with the Other Side, and not even sure what he was seeking, Bill Blatty reported that he had experimented with EVP (electronic voice phenomena) with reel-to-reel tape recordings and received unearthly voice communication. He started with a blank reel and set the tape recorder on slow and asked the question, *Does God exist?* Then he set the microphone to the highest setting, pushed the record button and waited three minutes. After the tape was replayed, a distinct male voice clearly spoke the word, *Lacey.* The second time he replayed the tape at a higher speed he heard the words, *Hope It,* words he believed referred to his original question. Some of his experiments produced phrases like, *I know what you are thinking, There's no space here,* and *Make them pray, Bill.*

Bill sent a copy of the original tape to a friend at Columbia University who ran it through a spectrograph, and the analysis revealed the voice couldn't be human. In order to create that effect, an artificial larynx would have had to been built and programmed to say those words. There was no logical explanation as to how a word like "Lacey" could change to "Hope It" when replayed at high speed.

Bill recently wrote another autobiography, *Finding Peter,* which included the strange events that have happened place in his home since the sudden death of his 19-year-old son, Peter. A chandelier dims and brightens on its own and other anomalies have taken place. These events confirm to him that his son is making contact from the Other Side.

The Knowing

Question: Explain what you mean by "The Knowing."

Answer: It's a feeling that overcomes me and I know that I'm right about something or someone. I'll give you two examples of it. My husband and I were at a casino in Reno, Nevada. As we sat at a bar next to some slot machines, an overwhelming feeling told me to play the slot machines nearest us. Finally I got up a put a quarter in it and it paid $100.

Another example of "The Knowing: a friend was visiting and wanted a glass of red wine. We sat on a light sage-green sofa as I envisioned her dog or mine would knock over the wine glass. It would shatter and stain the carpet and sofa. I immediately replaced her glass with one that wouldn't break.

Well, I guess some events can't be changed—you can alter events but the outcome is the same. One of the dogs jumped up on her lap and she spilled her red wine on herself and all over the sofa and carpet. But the plastic glass didn't shatter!

Sandy Hook Elementary Shooting

Question: I heard you on a radio talk show say that you knew something horrible was going to happen the morning of December 14, 2012 when twenty-year-old Adam Lanza shot and killed twenty young students and six adults. What did you sense?

Answer: That morning at 6:00 a.m. Mountain Time I woke up with a feeling of deep foreboding, sensing something evil was going to take place. It's the worst feeling I've ever had, which I can't begin to describe to you. I didn't know what was going to happen, but I knew it involved death of a people. As the morning progressed the feeling got worse until about 7:30 a.m. my time, 9:30 a.m. Eastern time when the shooting began.

There have been many conspiracy theories that Adam Lanza was not alone when he entered the school and shot children and adults that morning. My sense is we haven't been told the truth about the shooting there. It may takes years before we know what really happened there on December 14, 2012. You might find this odd, but the date 12 + 14 + 2012 equals the number 13, a number associated with the Illuminati. I've written at length about the number 13 in my book, *Mystic Revelations of Thirteen.*

Chapter Twelve

The Future

If you think you're too small to make a difference, try sleeping with a mosquito.—His Holiness The Dalai Lama

Conspiracy Theories

Question: You believe that humanity is controlled by a cabal that wants to rule the world. Can you elaborate on this conspiracy theory?

Answer: In the past fifteen years I've seen how more and more of our freedom is being taken away from us each day—laws passed under our noses. A great evil happened on 9/11/2001 when the World Trade Towers were allegedly brought down by Mid-Eastern terrorists taking control of two commercial airlines. One year before the event I had a terrifying dream. I stood before a giant apple tree full of apples and leaves, and then the leaves and apples began to fall very quickly from the tree and the entire tree was sucked into the ground and vanished. At the time I didn't understand this symbolic dream—however, I did realize that this realistic dream was a glimpse of an evil event sometime in the near future.

One year later, on September 11, 2001, after the World Trade Towers were brought down I realized the tree represented New York City, also known as "The Big Apple," and the apples and tree leaves falling from the tree's limbs represented the 2,985 souls who died that day. This dream was a warning that the events were orchestrated at least a year in advance and what we were told about the events didn't happen as the government told us. The Towers, including Building Seven that was never hit by a plane, were brought down by controlled demolition explosives. The planes were made to make us think they were responsible, but the truth is the Family of Dark planned this heinous deed to bring about a new war in the Mideast—Iraq.

Someday the truth will be known and the "evil doers" who planned 9-11 will be known and what a shock it will be to those who bought into their lies.

Question: I'm a big fan of Barbara Marciniak's channeled information from the teachings of the Pleiadians in her books, *Brings of the Dawn—Teachings from the Pleiadians, Family of Light,* and *Earth—Pleiadian Keys to the Living Library.* Why is the Family of Dark controlling children through sexual abuse and pornography?

Answer: Thank you for your question. These books are priceless and should be read and re-read to understand the wisdom we've been given by these highly evolved beings. Leaders around the world have been involved in the dark occult practices of sexual abuse with children for eons. They know children are innocent and can be controlled easily. Many leaders from around the globe, and I won't name them, particularly in the fields of politics, religion and education—those areas that are purportedly dedicated to children are part of a massive covert organization of pedophiles who use children for sex. It happens from one family member to another for generation—sex without love and sex for control. This is one of the darkest secrets of Family of Dark on our planet. The houses of the rich are riddled with this secret; sex with family members, sex for ritual abuse, sex for calling-in darkness and the dark Goddess, where no vibration of love exists, only a vibration of seeking power.

In these books, the Pleiadians say we must not run away from this realization to have light. You must learn about the power of darkness in order to understand the wounds and waywardness in the souls of these beings, who are desperately seeking something that was never given to them by their parents or by anyone else. This lack of love stays in their bloodline generation after generation. The wayward ones on your planet, whether murderers, rapists, pedophiles, or mass manipulators, are all devoid of love and do not know it. And so y our task of healing the planet will grow greater as the dark secrets of the world's ruling families and their dark occult practices are discovered.

Misuse of sexuality is not new. Child pornography and child slavery, the slavery of men and women around the globe, and the raping of men and women, have always been common. You have hidden the practice in your stories of Earth and do not study the subject in your classrooms. Perhaps you will consider studying the dark, having a course in your schools devoted to the dark misuse of power. As you educate your young, it is important to place the cards of darkness on the table. In many areas around the world, the dark forces are acknowledged and offerings are made, tokens left. Even in the practice of exorcising entities attached to humans, an offering of food or a piece of sweets is used to pull the entity into the offering.

We will see shocks and scandals the likes of which we have never seen before. Ideally we will wake up and see that what is happening in one country is happening everywhere.

Many indigenous people of your world were in touch with their multidimensional ancestors. They knew them through the dimensions, through time, and through their own blood. They also knew that they would live again and again, which is why in the development of their own cultures they planned ahead, sometimes for seven generations. They believe that what we do today effects the next seven generations, and it does! We are creating the future.

Your ancestors understood this principle, which has been deleted from your sacred texts.

Karma for Countries
Question: Do countries have karma like humans?

Answer: Definitely! We are now seeing revolts, uprisings, cries of vengeance, and anarchy, and many leaders fleeing their lands. Much of this anger and hate began eons ago and has never been settled. But killing is not the answer, and it will only create more karma for those people, groups and countries involved. Be proud of your lineage as a human. Find the oneness in your hearts to connect to the consciousness of all humans to begin the healing for Earth and all her creatures. Be kind, forgive and love others as you would want others to treat you.

Fairy Tales

Question: You have written some unnerving information for most of us, but why do you think we should hear the truth?

Answer: We've been handed sweet little fairy tales about our history. Most of the ancient myths and legends are based on fact handed down from generation to generation, yet much of our history remains hidden from us—we've been told we are alone in the universe, giants didn't roam the Earth, extraterrestrials didn't teach us advances sciences, UFOs aren't ET controlled, and modern homo sapiens suddenly appeared on the planet 100,000 years ago when in fact humans appeared on Earth as far back as a million years ago. Remember truth is knowledge. Certain groups have withheld the history of Earth and other sacred knowledge, knowing they can control us by lies and deceit. Humans are easily hoodwinked! The good news is people are awakening every day to the truth—it will set us free!!!

Dreams of a Cataclysmic Earth

Question: Weird things are happening to our planet—mysterious booms, sink holes worldwide, volcanoes suddenly erupting, weird weather globally, and animals and sea creatures dying. Are we being warned of the End Times?

Answer: At the age of seven shortly after I was chased home from school by a massive UFO, I began to have recurring nightmares of catastrophic events—volcanoes erupting, mega earthquakes, tsunami waves hitting coastal areas, and hurricane force winds hitting the planet. I have always know I was given glimpses of future events—by whom I don't know, but it's all happening now. We are in those times as foreseen by prophets and Indigenous elders worldwide. In today's world we have a separation sickness for nature. We have forgotten that everything is related and everything has a consciousness. We have become to connected to our electronic gadgets and have forgotten there is another world around us that contains the Living Library and the secrets to the elements and all of Earth's wisdom. Our ancestors and indigenous people have always known that everything is alive and has consciousness, and they honored everything. If they cut down a tree, they honored it in ceremony and prayer. If an animal was killed, it was honored and thanked for the life it was giving to the tribe.

In the world of today humanity has forgotten gratitude. We have forgotten to honor ourselves and all life as precious and part of the Great Creator of All Things. These Earth changes taking place now are to awaken us from our comatose state. Mother Earth wants to survive from the poisons and toxins we continue to put into her body. We remove precious metals from our Mother—uranium, gold, silver, crystals, oil, that holds our energy grid together. Everything on our planet has a purpose, yet we don't understand that connection. Once the link is broken it causes disastrous consequences for all life.

Already we are seeing those consequences. Fish in the Pacific Ocean are vanishing at an alarming rate, sea stars are dying and melting from California to Alaska from unknown causes, seals are starving. Is it from the radiation from Fukushima, pollution in our oceans or have we begun to see the consequences of overfishing the oceans? I believe it's all the above.

Lessen Earth Changes

Question: Can we stop or lessen the Earth changes in our future?
Answer: If we as species make quality of life the number one priority in our lives by honoring the quality of Earth's life, there will be very few Earth changes upon this planet. But most of us are too concerned with our electronic devices, how many clothes are in our closets, and how many cars are in our garages. We are addicted modern day electronic gadgets that have a detrimental effect on the

sentient beings of our planet. If we don't change—if we do not shift our values and realize that without Mother Earth we could not be here--then Earth, in her need to survive and her need to reach a higher frequency, will bring about a cleansing for balance. Maybe then everyone, and not just a few, will awaken to what's really going on. But no matter what, a new world is coming. If we make the change, and honor our planet, the Earth changes will be gradual and not sudden. It's our choice to love and honor our planet now.

It is time for prayer, meditation, and intention. My teachers, Corbin Harney (1920-2007) Spiritual Leader of the Western Shoshone Nation, and Ed McGaa "Eagle Man," Lakota Sioux Ceremonial Leader and Author, have told me the importance of prayer, reconnecting and honoring Mother Earth and all sentient beings. Corbin said, "We have to come back to the Native way of life. The Native Way is to pray to for everything. Our Mother Earth is very important. We can't just misuse her and think she's going to continue. Now, I don't think we're going to be able to change until we can get our spiritual people together. We have to start joining together to pray. We all have to try to keep our Mother Earth clean. We are going to have to join hands together the best way we can and do one thing…PRAY."

In Carol Schaefer's book, *Grandmothers Counsel the World*, she writes that on October 17, 2004, Thirteen Indigenous Grandmothers from around the world intuitively heard the urgent call to gather and pray for Earth Mother in Phoenicia, New York. They came from the Amazon rain forest, the Arctic Circle of North America, the great forest of the American Northwest, the vast plains of North America, the highlands of Central America, the Black Hills of South Dakota, the mountains of Oaxaca, the desert of the American Southwest, the mountains of Tibet, and the rain forest of central Africa.

When Grandmother Clara of the Amazon was visited by the Star Beings, she was told that the Galactic Dawn began in 2012—a mass awakening of humanity to our cosmic origins and intergalactic relationship. She also said, "What I see today in the world is a lot of darkness and a few points of light trying to illuminate us as we go through the dark tunnel of our Age. We Grandmothers here are hold each other's hands, illuminating the path, so that we can bring health to this Mother Earth and heal the wounds She is suffering from, wounds made by ignorant men, ignorant of the truth of the Light and the Creator. The message from the Beings of the Stars is that it is necessary for everyone to open their hearts to the truth of Spirit, of the Spirit World, as it is this truth that will lead us to our salvation."

The Grandmothers say that the Earth's changes will bring about an awakening of spiritual consciousness for humanity. Only when we drop our egos can Spirit be heard.

Planet X aka Nibiru

Question: Do you believe there's a Planet X that will shift Earth's poles in the near future? *Answer:* A few years ago I noticed a large object near the setting sun. I can't say this was Planet X, a failed star or brown dwarf, which travels through our solar system every 3,600 years, but I know that something in our solar systems is affecting all the planets according to NASA. In a June 18, 2012 BBC documentary on Nibiru, now posted on YouTube, the Inuits of the Arctic regions have noticed changes in the stars and where the sun sets. They hunt and observe the changes in the weather, the stars, the sun and they believe the Earth has shifted, tilted or as they put it, "wobbled" to the north and they all agree "Their sky has changed!"

The elders maintain the Sun doesn't rise where it used to, they have longer daylight to hunt and the Sun is higher than it used to be and warms up quicker than before. The elders who were interviewed across the north all said the same thing, their sky has changed.

The stars the Sun and the Moon have all changed affecting the temperature, even affecting the way the wind blows, it is becoming increasingly hard to predict the weather, something that is a must on the Arctic. The elders all agree, they believe the Earth has shifted, wobbled or tilted to the North.

So to answer your question, I believe in cause and effect, and I believe Planet X could be causing part of the changes taking place on our planet now as well as the human caused planet changes—fracking that pulls oil and gas out of Mother Earth, her lifeblood, the poison we are putting into Her, the microwave technology, CERN's particle accelerators experiments conducted in Switzerland and God knows what other technological experiments are being conducted by the military and governments.

At CERN, the European Organization for Nuclear Research, physicists and engineers are probing the fundamental structure of the universe. They use the world's largest and most complex scientific instruments to study the basic constituents of matter—the fundamental particles. The particles are made to collide together at close to the speed of light. The process gives the physicists clues about how the particles interact, and provides insights into the fundamental laws of nature. It is said that CERN will conduct an experiment the fall of 2015 where 14 trillion electron volts or terra electrons will be produced. What effect will it have on our planet?

Mysterious Booms and Horn Sounds Worldwide

Question: Earth Mysteries Investigator Linda Moulton Howe has been on Coast to Coast AM radio show reporting on the mysterious booms and horn-like sounds heard worldwide lately. Any idea what is causing this?

Answer: Deep-core Earth movement. I've noticed that whenever the booms are heard, a powerful earthquake follows within days somewhere in the world. It could be methane gas and other gases being released which created a "sky quake." In 2015 the Urals of Siberia, Russia have experienced sinkholes forming everywhere. One theory suggests methane gas released from the melting permafrost of Siberia has caused explosions and the sinkholes.

I've listened to the recorded sounds posted on YouTube and it sounds like a train trying to brake or gears that need oiling. I think the Earth rotation is slowing—she's putting on her brakes.

Methane Gas worldwide

Question: Do you think the methane is contributing to the deaths of millions of fish worldwide, birds dropping dead from the sky and other animals dying suddenly?

Answer: March 2015 it was reported by the Idaho Fish and Game that 2,000 snow geese fell from the sky dead. I've tried to find out what the tests on the geese revealed from Fish and Game Department in Eastern Idaho, but they won't tell me anything. Strange! Reports of sea lions off the coast of California has been in the news lately, sardines have simply vanished from the Pacific and I just learned that Copper River Salmon from Oregon has almost vanished. I was told that one-hundred boats when out to catch the fish and only four boats returned with salmon.

What is happening to the ecology of our oceans? Some believe the radiation in the Pacific from Fukushima has cause the die-off of many fragile species, and others believe methane gas is rising up from the ocean floor, which poisons animals similar to carbon monoxide by asphyxiation. This is what I believe is causing the mass fish kills and bird falling from the skies, and even dead sheep, elk and deer have been in the news lately. The released gas from many parts of the world is taking place from when prior pole shifts forced rock layers atop one another. Methane gas released is found in the stretch zones where these rock layers are being pulled apart. Another place this is taking place is in the Ural of Russia where sinkholes are forming.

Feeling Strange Stuff

Question: I'm experiencing some really strange things lately—sleeplessness, dizziness, not focused. Is this something others are experiencing now?

Answer: First of all, please check with your doctor to determine your symptoms aren't something serious. But to answer your question, I've received emails from people stating they are feeling weird as if something is going to happen. The "symptoms" usually go on for a couple of weeks at a time and then subside, happening again as cosmic, solar activity and earth changes increase. We are going from the fourth dimension or world into the fifth world and as we do so we will feel our DNA changing. Everything is changing now. Many people are releasing their karmic and emotional agreements, re-evaluating their beliefs and their choices in relationships, jobs, and where they live that no longer works for their soul agreement.

I find that meditation, spending a day at the mountains, by a river, lake, will calm anxiety and energize me again. Any moving water such as rivers, the ocean, waterfalls, contain negative ions (positive ions make you feel irritable such as dry winds) that have proven to be beneficial to the body. Mountains also have negative-charged ions. HERE IS A LIST OF SOME OF THE STRANGE SYMPTOMS PEOPLE HAVE EXPERIENCED:

1. Sugar/chocolate cravings.

2. Unfamiliar eating patterns.

3. Weird sleep patterns, strong need for extra sleep and naps.

4. Pressure, pain, swirling and drilling sensations around solar plexus area.

6. Pressure and moving sensations

7. Headaches.

8. Hearing strange sounds. People are reporting hearing the same kind of buzzing "metallic/mechanical" yet somehow really pleasant "otherworldly" sounds and also a hum that reminds them of "sounds of the spheres".

8. Heightened sensitivity and increased psychic awareness of everything around you.

9. Intensified senses, especially the sense of smell.

10. Electrical malfunctions, like lights and computers, when you get near them.

12. Being out of focus as if being inside a movie.

13. Loss of balance and vertigo.

14. Waves of intense emotions.

15. Enhanced ADD-like symptoms or dyslexia.

16. Confusion and forgetfulness.

17. Strange, unfamiliar sensations in the body.

18. Extra-fast healing of the body.

20. Heightened synchronicities with people and events.

21. Instant manifesting of thoughts into reality.

22. Intensified visuals in meditations and vivid dreams.

23. Time shifts and loss of sense of time.

25. Sudden revelations and inspiration.

Trusting our Intuition

Question: How do we trust our intuition and prepare for earth changes?

Answer: Our ancient ancestors didn't possess cell phones, TV, radios to warn them of hurricanes, tornadoes, warring tribes, and fierce animals, but they did use their innate sixth sense, which we all have. The problem today is we have become too attached to our physical world and have forgotten another world coexists with ours. Everyone has this ability to sense earthquake and other natural disasters—it can be an inner voice that warns us not to do something, and pets have been known to detect the compression waves or ULFs (ultra low frequency) before a major earthquake. Some humans also detect ULFs and feel dizzy, have headaches and nausea before a big earthquake. Horses and cattle also become nervous before a disaster—tornadoes, hurricanes, volcanic eruptions and earthquakes. Rocks grinding together within the Earth can create piezo electric or "earthquake lights." Birds often become strangely quiet.

There are always signs and warning from Mother Earth. I've noticed on the government USGS earthquake monitor site that swarm earthquake usually indicate something is building, and a powerful earthquake usually takes place. Earthquakes usually happen early morning and on the Full Moon. I've also observed earthquakes when a large solar eruption takes place and Earth gets hit with a CME (coronal mass ejection). We can all learn to trust our intuition, disconnect as much as possible from electronic gadget that interfere with our intuition and reconnect with Mother Earth. As to be guided and warned of major disasters. Mother Earth and your angels and guides are listening!

Where are we headed?

Question: There is so much gloom and doom on our planet now and predictions of the end times, but where do you think we are headed.

Answer: We make our future and it is up to us to change the dark road we are currently on. As far as cleaning up the environment, no one is going to save us from our own mess. We created it, and otherworldly beings want to see if we can awaken in time. I have been shown a vision of Earth far into the future where humanity will not be consumed in the material, where they will honor all life and live in balance with Mother Earth. Humans will wear simple clothes—no one will have more than another. Animals will not be abused, but honored and cherish just like human children. Children will be taught Earth Wisdom—that everything is connected and has a consciousness. There will be technology but it will be in harmony with Mother Earth and only the elements will be harnessed to create natural energy. No more greed, no more hate, no more wars, and no pollution. It won't be a perfect world, but it will be a world of wonder and beautiful where forests have returned, the creatures of the earth are plentiful and healthy and the waters of the Earth run clean again. The population of the planet will have been greatly decreased, and it will take a long time for a great many souls to reincarnate again.

Right now, this moment, you are being given an extraordinary opportunity to advance spiritually. What you do, what you think, what you say, will imprint your soul and determine what you will be in your next incarnation. Take this opportunity to help Mother Earth, speak your truth and love and honor all life!

The atoms of our bodies are traceable to stars that manufactured them in their cores and exploded these enriched ingredients across our galaxy, billions of years ago. For this reason, we are biologically connected to every other living thing in the world. We are chemically connected to all molecules on Earth. And we are atomically connected to all atoms in the universe. We are not figuratively, but literally stardust. — Astrophysicist Neil deGrasse Tyson

Epilogue

My wish is that everyone reading this book will reconnect to Mother Earth and Earth Wisdom like the Ancient Ones and indigenous people throughout the world. The Lakota Sioux have a saying, *Mitakuye Oyasin*, which means, *we are related to all things*. Here's the amazing part about the saying—it's true! All living organisms store genetic information using the same molecules—DNA and RNA. Written in the genetic code of these molecules is compelling evidence of the shared ancestry with all living things.

I'd like to believe we haven't reached the point of no return to heal our Mother Earth, and that together we will turn things around. It takes team work and speaking out against injustices taking place on our planet. Don't be a spiritual couch potato and say you are only one person because it takes many single persons united in one consciousness to create massive change on Earth.

As Earthkeepers practicing Earth Wisdom we can start by seeing the moment as perfect and then we can change anything we want. The Inca Wisdomkeepers say that once we step outside of time into infinity, the past and future disclose themselves to us—everything becomes clear. Psychic Edgar Cayce said that 12 billion years ago, the energy gestalt we call God, existed in an unmanifested void, and so it decided to experience itself, and produced the big bang, forming all matter in our universe and other universes. God continued to explore itself through all forms of matter—worlds, planets, stars, animals, insects, rocks, water and all beings. It was both omnipresent and omniscient, and so were all its manifestations. If such a scenario is true, how can we deny our power and our connection to the Creator of all things?

As my friend, Corbin Harney taught, "As we all know, our water is going to be pretty precious. I think we all realize this today. I talk about this, and I hope people out there will continue to talk about this, and not be behind the bush like I was. I used to be behind the bush with what I know; I never could come out from behind the bush. Now it's time for us all to come out from behind the bush and start hollering. I don't care how we do it, as long as we do it together."

Like Corbin, I used to be behind the bush, afraid to speak my mind and tell people of the things I've been shown in visions and dreams through the years. No one was listening years ago. Now it's time for everyone to be courageous and step forward as Earthkeepers and Lightkeepers about the abuse of our planet and the changes taking place. If we don't use our voices, all will be lost.

Shortly after my seventh birthday I was shown vivid dreams of cataclysmic Earth changes—tsunami waves hitting coastal shores, volcanoes erupting, earthquakes shaking the land and ferocious winds. Since that time I've been warned of earthquakes, solar flares and even volcanic eruptions. I'm not sure where these visions come from—spirit guides, my guardian angels or interdimensional beings, but I do know it's true and real and I must trust the information. My visions are taking place at this time, and my sense is that something momentous is about to happen to our world.

In Dr. Ardy Sixkiller Clarke's book, *Sky People,* she interviewed Maya elders and indigenous people of Belize and Guatemala, and many of them said the Sky People warned them of a time of great change. They have been told that there will be wars and Earth shaking, that we are living in the fourth world, but a fifth world is coming, and now it's too late to stop it. They have been told that many sad things are about to happen to Earth. There will be signs in the heavens if people will take the time to look skyward, but the elders say people are too busy to look.

One Maya elder told her that, "This is the fourth world, Señora. It has been destroyed before. Each time, people were careless with the Earth. There is a reason why we are here. We were placed on this planet to look after it. We have been allowed to evolve as a people [the Maya], but we have not been able to perform the task given to us. A day is coming when we must answer for our disregard of our mission. On that day, the Earth will be turned upside down. They [Sky People] warn us that we must prepare for the future."

Another Maya elder told Dr. Clarke, "They [Sky People] said the Earth is changing and that a new world will come. They said there will be wars and Earth shaking. We are living in the fourth world, but a fifth world is coming. It is too late to stop it. I am supposed to tell the people to get ready. The four horsemen will come first. When these horsemen appear, the fourth world will end and the fifth world will begin."

These changes don't surprise me because I have expected them for many decades and watched the signs in the heavens and on Earth—UFO, orbs, mysterious booms heard world, giant cracks forming in Africa, Russia and in California, sea creatures and birds dying, and other anomalies. I know there will be other signs as Earth changes escalate in the coming years with extreme weather, the moon, stars and sun not in their normal positions, earthquakes in places not known for earthquake activity, sink holes forming, increased volcanic activity and strange lights in the sky.

When humans return to Earth mindfulness and hold our planet and all living creatures in the highest reverence, then we have taken the next step in our spiritual evolution. We will discover ways to live in harmony with our environment instead of destroying it and then Mother Earth will respond in kind—our thoughts and actions are reflected in her.

It's no coincidence that film director James Cameron's epic 2009 movie, *Avatar*, became a mega hit. The movie focused on a powerful environmental message that the senseless expansion and destruction of our environment has a butterfly effect. It affects all life on Earth. What the movie conveyed to audiences was it's time for humanity to open our eyes and hearts and see the world around us, the network of energy that flows through all living things on Mother Earth.

It's time to say we've had enough of this insanity and disrespect for our Mother Earth. It's time to practice and live *ayni,* and not only the Earth, but the universe will respond in kind to our actions. Time to walk in balance on the Earth and revere all things as divine, and created by Great Spirit or God. When we awaken to the unseen world, the spirit elements, and beings that surround our world and interact with us daily, we will have reached a perfect place of peace, grace and understanding. But we will need to drop our egos like the purity of animals, and stop thinking that we are superior to all other life. We are equal to all.

Spiritual leader Corbin Harney reminded us, "Always offer something to what you get off the land. Bless what you get off Mother Earth. Bless the water. Talk to it, keep it alive, keep it moving, keep the spirit in the water moving. If you talk to it and bless it, it really keeps the water happy, gives it strength."

We must teach our children a new way of living, in order to ensure future generations will have a beautiful Earth to enjoy and the abundance the Creator has given us. The Grandmothers tell us it is important to teach the children of the world how to humbly pray to the rocks, the trees, the sky, the mountains, the sacred waters, the birds, and all animals. Like the Grandmothers, Ed McGaa and Corbin, I am also deeply concerned about the younger generation and their future. The younger people have become so addicted to technology, their cell phones, video games, texting, they have forgotten the natural world, the real world—it's sad for them and humanity and sad for Mother Earth. Humanity has become lost in technology and the real world—the nature world. How will most of us survive if a great catastrophe should befall our planet? How will the young people survive without Earth Wisdom? That's why we must teach them the knowledge of Earth. Indigenous tribes who continue to practice the natural way will survive because this has been their way of life for eons. They understand the spirit elements and the signs Mother Earth provides. They listen with open hearts—unlike most of us who have closed our hearts and myopic minds.

Corbin believed it is very important to do the ceremonies and prayers. It's very important for all of us to get together again and again to honor Earth. He said, "Some of you go to church and pray together. That is very important, and it's what we must do. We have to pray to the sun, the Earth, the water, and to the air. I hope that we will all pick up this message that I'm putting out, so that we can have a cleaner life, and so the younger generation can continue on."

We are connected to the Great Mystery. Through my own paranormal and spiritual experiences I've learned there is so much more to life than what our normal senses perceive. There are other realities and life forms that coexist with us in other realities. There are ghosts, spirits, angels, fairies, and deities that reside in our world—mostly unseen. Instead of having closed eyes, we need to open our eyes and minds to other possibilities, other realities, and realize that nothing is impossible, and everything is possible.

We are fortunate to have taken on physical bodies to experience life at its fullest, to see with our physical eyes a sunset, a brilliant red sunrise, a rainbow arched across the sky, and an aurora borealis lighting up the night sky in vivid colors. Life is a circle, as the ancients taught, and everything returns to the Oneness of life.

As Earth changes increase, our bodies will feel the vibrational change. There are huge dynamics taking place within and on Mother Earth, and every living thing will be touched by those changes. If we believe the Hopi and that we are in the Purification Times, then the Prophecy Rock tell us that we have a choice. Will we save Mother Earth or watch her perish? Together, united, we can make a difference, and if you don't believe consciousness can affect change through intent and prayer, consider this: two of NOAAs (National Oceanic and Atmospheric Administrations) space weather satellites known as GOES-8 and GOES-10 that monitor Earth's geomagnetic field picked up a huge spike during the September 11, 2001 attack on the World Trade buildings, and several days after the attacks. Many theorized the spike indicated there were stress waves caused by mass human emotion on Earth's geomagnetic field. GOES-8, orbiting 22, 300 miles above the equator that day, detected a surge that topped out at nearly 50 units (nano testlas), higher than any previous recording. The time was 9 a.m. eastern standard time, 15 minutes after the first plane hit the World Trade Center and about minutes before the second impact.

Our thoughts, our fears, our anger, our love, our hate, go directly into Mother Earth. She feels us, and we feel her. If the majority of Earth people are locked in fear, where do you think that negative emotion goes? It's pure energy and it goes into the ether and into Mother Earth.

When we begin to understand the divinity, the cosmology of all life, we will no longer take our beautiful planet for granted, the Grandmothers tell us. They say in these days, when the prophecies are being fulfilled, we are the ones who will determine whether or not we will destroy our Mother Earth and ourselves. Each us have an obligation to decide whether or not to live in harmony and with a selfless love for the benefit of all. Not only do we have an obligation to ourselves but to future generations still unborn.

WHAT WILL OUR LEGACY BE FOR FUTURE GENERATIONS—DESTRUCTION OF MOTHER EARTH OR A WORLD OF BEAUTY AND BALANCE?

The Grandmothers say it is important to create a more personal sense of connection by holding rituals, ceremonies, and festivals. It is then that we speak directly to the spirit elements and Mother Earth. Ritual engages the spirit of a place, a circuit of energy in which the entire cosmos participates. There was a time, the Grandmothers remind us, when all of our ancestors revered Earth and used ceremonies to hold Earth's balance. Today, that balance no longer exists.

"Prayer is the greatest thing I have as I walk upon this Earth," Grandmother Agnes of Oregon says. 'I am nothing without the Creator. When you have the Creator with you, you have the force behind you, and negativity doesn't take over you, even in the dreamtime. You can't change even your children, except through prayer. Prayer is a duty that has been handed down from the Ancient Ones that went before us."

To be an Earthkeeper start with self- love and radiate that love outward—love Mother Earth, all her creation, and love all humanity. Eagle Man says, "Our survival is dependent on the realization that Mother Earth is a truly holy being, that all things in this world are holy and must not be violated, and that we must share and be generous with one another. Think of your fellow men and women as holy people who were put here by the Great Spirit. Think of being related to all things! With this philosophy in mind as we go on with our environmental ecology efforts, our search for spirituality, and our quest for peace, we will be far more successful when we truly understand the Indians' respect for Mother Earth."

In these times of great change, trust your intuition, trust what the creatures tell you, trust the sky, the ocean, the elements, the insects, the birds, the sea creatures to warn you when Earth starts to move in a big way. Speak to Mother Earth and ask her to guide you to safety areas—she hears your words.

The most astonishing fact is that you are made up of stars, nebulas, galaxies, black holes—the very fabric of the universe. In other words—you are literally STARDUST, the atoms and molecules of the universe. Now it's time to start acting like the remarkable spiritual beings we were created to be by honoring Mother Earth and all life.

Astronomer, cosmologist and astrophysicist Carl Sagan (1934-1996) left us with his beautiful words of wisdom in his book, *The Pale Blue Dot,* "If you look at Earth from space you see a dot, that's here. That's home. That's us! It underscores the responsibility to deal more kindly and compassionately with one another and to preserve and cherish that pale blue dot, the only home we've ever known. Thank you all."

As the Lakota Sioux have always known, *Mitakuye Oyasin—we are all related!*

Brothers and sisters, we must go back to some of the old ways if we are going to truly save our Mother Earth and bring back the natural beauty that every person seriously needs, especially in this day of vanishing species, vanishing rain forests, overpopulation, poisoned waters, acid rain, a thinning ozone layer, drought, rising temperatures, and weapons of complete annihilation. —Ed McGaa "Eagle Man" Oglala Sioux Ceremonial Leader

Living Earth Wisdom by Ed McGaa "Eagle Man" and Betsey Lewis

Bring back the natural harmony that humans once enjoyed.

Honor your body, your living temple, with natural food, sleep and exercise.

Love and forgive all. Rid yourself of prejudice.

Practice real truth each day.

Take time each day to pray, visualize, meditate, intend a new world, a healed planet for all.

Gratitude: appreciate your life, the planet and all blessings that come into your life.

Practice ceremony—the indigenous way or your own way. Take time to practice reverence. Take time to hug a tree, smell flowers, and give thanks to all life. Remove your shoes and talk to Mother Earth. Listen to the frogs and crickets toning and anchoring Earth's grid. Find moving water, and feel the negative ions. Feel the elemental spirits.

Be kind to animals, and give thanks to the animals you eat!

Honor and cherish children.

Teach your children Earth Wisdom, and how to honor life.

Disconnect as much as possible from negative news, cell phones, computers, television and electronics. Reconnect with Mother Earth.

Be brave and courageous enough to take a stand and make a commitment. Let your voice be heard.

Share with others and be less materialistic.

Be magnanimous of self and charitable to others.

Recycle, recycle, recycle everything! Clean up trash and plastic in city parks and national parks. If you pack it in, pack it out!

Trust your intuition, trust Earth Mother and trust the creatures to warn you when the planet begins to move.

Laugh and love more. Practice compassion.

Find solitude in natural sounds of nature and soothing music that heals. Music is a healing vibration.

Be kind to yourself as the powerful spiritual being you are.

Bibliography

Breytenbach, Anna. Award-winning documentary, *The Animal Communicator* (Dec. 2013)

Carroll, Lee and Jan Tober. *The Indigo Children: The New Kids Have Arrived* (1999: Hay House)

Clarke, Ardy Sixkiller. *Sky People: Untold Stries of Alien Encoutners in Mesoamerica (*Pompton Plains, NJ: New Page Book 2015).

Harney, Corbin. *The Way It Is* (Nevada City, NV: Blue Dolphin Publishing, Inc. 1995).

Losey, Meg Blackburn. *The Children of Now* (Franklin Lake, NJ: Career Press 2007).

McGaa, Ed. *Mother Earth Spirituality (*New York, NY: HarperSan Franciso 1990), *Rainbow Tribe (*New York, NY: HarperSanFrancisco 1992) *Spirituality for America, Creator's Code.*

Roberts, Jane. *The Seth Material* (New York, NY: Bantam 1976) and *Seth Speaks: The Eternal Validity of the Soul (*San Rafael, CA: Amber-Allen Publishing 1972 and 1994).

Schaeffer, Carol. *Grandmothers Counsel the World: Women Elders Offer Their Vision of Our Planet* (Boston, MA: Trumpeter Books 2006).

About Betsey Lewis

Betsey Lewis, an internationally-renowned psychic/medium, talk show host of Rainbow Vision Network and earth mysteries investigator, inherited the gift of prophecy from her mother.

For over forty years Betsey has investigated UFO sightings, cattle mutilations, angels, aliens, and other Earth mysteries. She practices Reiki, Kriya Yoga, astrology, tarot and numerology, and regressive hypnosis. She spent ten years with Native American ceremonial and spiritual leaders like Spiritual Leader of the Shoshone Nation Corbin Harney and Lakota Sioux Ceremonial Leader and author Ed McGaa "Eagle Man" learning Earthkeeper ways while attending pow-wows, healing ceremonies, vision quests, and sweat lodge ceremonies in the Idaho, California, Oregon, Canada and Central America.

Betsey has hosted the Rainbow Vision Network since 2009, featuring bestselling authors and renowned investigators into the paranormal and metaphysical world. She has been a guest on the Dr. Michael Show, Idaho's KTVB Noon show, KIVI Morning show, and numerous radio talk shows including Coast to Coast AM, KTALK's The Fringe, X-Zone, and Ground Zero Talk Radio. Betsey was a keynote speaker at the 2012 UFO Conference in Alamo, Nevada, near Area 51.

Published nonfiction books include: *Earth Energy—Return to Ancient Wisdom, Mystic Revelations of Thirteen—The Key to Earth's Destiny; Angels, Aliens and Prophecy—The Connection, Angels, Aliens and Prophecy II—The Angel-Alien Agenda,* and three spiritual books for young adults and children—*Alexander Phoenix and The Seven Sacred Virtues*, *The Story of Rainbow Eyes,* and *A Worm Named Sherm.*

Betsey lives in Southwestern Idaho with her husband and her beloved dog and cat. Betsey's website: www.betseylewis.com. She maintains the popular *Earth News1 blog* on her website.

Made in the USA
San Bernardino, CA
07 October 2016